THE SIMPLE KNITTING
GUIDE FOR BEGINNERS

HAYADAN STEPHANSON

INTRODUCTION

Welcome to the world of knitting—a delightful journey that intertwines creativity, relaxation, and the joy of crafting with your own hands. This book, "The Simple Knitting Guide for Beginners," is your comprehensive companion on the path to becoming a skilled and confident knitter. Whether you're a complete novice or someone looking to refine their skills, this guide is designed to demystify the art of knitting and provide you with the knowledge and confidence to embark on your knitting adventure.

In the vast realm of crafting, knitting stands out as a timeless and rewarding skill. The rhythmic motion of needles, the soft textures of yarn, and the endless possibilities of creating beautiful, handmade items make knitting an art form accessible to all. This book aims to be your trusted mentor, guiding you through the fundamentals, techniques, and projects that will not only build your skills but also ignite your passion for this age-old craft.

The Beginning of Your Journey

Chapter 1 sets the stage for your knitting journey, offering a detailed exploration of the essential tools and resources needed to dive into this fulfilling craft. From selecting the right yarn to choosing the perfect needles, you'll gain insights into the foundational elements that contribute to a successful knitting experience. Ten General Tips will pave the way for a smoother start, addressing common challenges faced by beginners and providing practical solutions to enhance your knitting endeavors.

Mastering the Basics

Chapter 2 delves into the core techniques every knitter should master. Beginning with the fundamental Cast On, you'll progress through Basic Knit Stitches and conclude with the crucial Bind Off. Along the way, you'll find step-by-step instructions and helpful illustrations to ensure that you grasp each technique with confidence. To reinforce your learning, a Practice Project awaits you at the end of this chapter—an opportunity to apply your newfound skills and create something tangible.

Bringing Your Skills to Life

Chapter 3 introduces a variety of beginner-friendly projects, allowing you to apply your skills in real-time. From Hats and Scarves to Afghans and Cushion Covers, each project is designed to progressively challenge you while providing the satisfaction of completing beautiful and functional items. The diverse range of projects ensures there's something for everyone, whether you're knitting for yourself or creating heartfelt gifts for loved ones.

Exploring Beyond the Basics

Chapter 4 takes you a step further with Combination Beginner Knit Projects, offering a mix of creativity and skill-building. Explore the world of Ponchos and Vests, create cozy Socks, and add a personal touch to your coffee routine with Coffee Mug Coozies. These projects introduce new elements and techniques, allowing you to expand your repertoire and build confidence in tackling more complex endeavors.

Transitioning to Intermediate Knitting

As you gain proficiency, Chapter 5 prepares you for the intermediate level. Eight Tips for Success as an Intermediate Knitter offer valuable insights to navigate this stage effectively. Building on this knowledge, you'll then delve into Intermediate Knitting Stitches and Projects, providing a seamless transition to more intricate patterns and designs.

Crafting Your Own Masterpieces

In the CONCLUSION, we reflect on the journey you've embarked upon and celebrate the newfound skills and creativity you've cultivated. As you flip through the pages of this guide, you'll not only discover the joy of knitting but also unlock the potential to create personalized, handmade treasures that tell your unique story.

"The Simple Knitting Guide for Beginners" is more than just a book; it's a companion on your creative voyage. Join us as we unravel the beauty of knitting, one stitch at a time, and empower you to craft a world of warmth, style, and heartfelt gifts with your own two hands. Let the journey begin!

A Journey of Discovery

Embarking on your knitting journey is akin to setting sail on a voyage of self-discovery. As you immerse yourself in Chapter 1, you'll find that choosing the right supplies is not just a practical consideration but an essential aspect of personal expression. Uncover the nuances of various yarn types, colors, and textures, and understand how the selection of needles can influence the outcome of your projects. The journey begins with the careful curation of tools that resonate with your style and vision.

The voyage continues with Ten General Tips, addressing the common stumbling blocks that can impede a beginner's progress. From unraveling the mysteries of gauge and tension to troubleshooting common mistakes, these tips serve as navigational beacons, guiding you through potential challenges with ease. Prepare to set sail confidently, armed with knowledge that will smooth the initial waves of your knitting adventure.

Weaving the First Stitches

In Chapter 2, the world of knitting unfolds as you learn the foundational techniques that form the basis of countless knitting endeavors. Casting On marks the inception of your creations, and as you progress through Basic Knit Stitches, the language of knitting becomes second nature. The importance of a proper Bind Off is unveiled, ensuring your projects culminate in a polished and professional finish.

To solidify your understanding of these techniques, a Practice Project awaits you at the end of the chapter. This hands-on experience not only reinforces your skills but also serves as a tangible testament to your progress. The satisfaction of completing your first project is a milestone in your knitting journey, a testament to your newfound abilities.

From Yarn to Wearable Art

Chapter 3 opens the door to a world of possibilities as you embark on your first set of projects. Each item, from Hats and Scarves to Afghans and Cushion Covers, is carefully curated to provide a diverse range of experiences. Discover the joy of transforming simple stitches into functional and aesthetically pleasing items. The projects in this chapter are more than mere creations; they are the embodiment of your creativity, each stitch a brushstroke in the canvas of your knitting story.

As you navigate through the projects, you'll find a sense

of accomplishment that goes beyond the finished item. Knitting becomes a meditative practice, allowing you to immerse yourself in the rhythmic flow of stitches and the tactile sensation of yarn passing through your fingers. This chapter is not just about creating objects; it's about weaving the threads of your imagination into wearable art.

Beyond the Basics

Chapter 4 introduces you to the realm of combination projects, where you'll merge your newfound skills into more complex designs. Ponchos and Vests offer an opportunity to explore garment construction, while Socks and Coffee Mug Coozies infuse your creations with practicality and style. These projects serve as stepping stones, challenging you to embrace creativity and develop a deeper understanding of the craft.

Navigating the Intermediate Waters

Chapter 5 signifies a transition to the intermediate level, a stage where you spread your wings and explore more intricate patterns and techniques. The eight tips provided are like a compass, guiding you through the nuances of this stage with confidence. Armed with this knowledge, you'll delve into Intermediate Knitting Stitches and Projects, where you'll encounter the joy of creating intricate lacework, textured patterns, and more sophisticated designs.

A Tapestry of Creativity

In the CONCLUSION, take a moment to reflect on the tapestry of creativity you've woven throughout the chapters. Your journey doesn't end here; it's a continuous thread that connects each stitch, project, and lesson. The skills you've acquired and the projects you've completed are not just items to cherish but symbols of your evolving passion for knitting.

As you embark on this journey through "The Simple Knitting Guide for Beginners," envision your hands transforming skeins of yarn into cherished items, your creativity expressed through each stitch. Join us as we unravel the layers of this craft, revealing a world where simplicity meets artistry, and where every knitted piece tells a story—a story that is uniquely yours. Let the yarn guide you, and may this book be the companion that enriches your knitting adventure.

CONTENTS

Chapter 1: How to Start Knitting—Supplies and Resources

So, you have decided to join in the fun and crazy world of knitting? Welcome! Fair warning: you will get addicted to this amazing hobby. It is super fun and at times pretty overwhelming, especially for those just starting out. If you have gone down the knitting aisles at your local craft store staring at the endless rows of yarn and needles, you may be wondering where to even start. Choosing the right supplies to start with will save you tons of time, not to mention save you tons of money. There will be plenty of time to share tips and techniques on how to knit and purl like a professional, but to start you on the path with confidence, this chapter is geared towards getting you set up with the right supplies and resources for all your future beginning (and some intermediate) projects.

Ten General Tips

1. Do not go overboard in the crafting aisle.

It is beautiful, right? All the fluffy balls of yarn and shiny needles glittering in front of you? Do you envision yourself sitting comfortably, knitting with your beautiful needles, and creating gorgeous gifts? As you wander down the aisle, lightly passing your fingertips over the differently textured wools, you picture all the beautiful crafts you will be making for your friends and family. And before you know it, your cart is full of so many things; you do not remember them hopping into your cart. Several hundred dollars later and crafting room or box overflowing with new toys, it hits you that you have no clue what to start with or what you want to do. Or you start on a project and hate the way aluminum needles feel in your hand, but every time you touch the bamboo needles your friend uses, you swoon. You have a pile of notions you never touch but are always running back to the store to grab just one more of that one thing you use all the time. Save yourself the heartache and hassle, pick up a few of the basics to start, and then add on as you try new techniques or tools.

2. Save your money... in the beginning.

The pretty, sparkly, and colorful yarn is attractive. When it is soft or has a great texture, you just want to run your hands over it again and again. The problem is most of the time that yarn is expensive. As you begin learning, you will be knitting and remove stitches, creating a lot of wear and tear on the yarn. All the pretty glitter and texture will be shredded. Your yarn will tangle—not a fun way to start your knitting experience. You are going to stretch out your first few yarns, so plan on investing in a good synthetic yarn that is inexpensive. Save those pretty yarns for when you are more experienced. Part of the joy of your later projects will be running to the store to pick up a flashy, fun, funky ball of yarn and revel in the joy of working with it, preserving the character of the fibers. Test your skills on cheap yarns so you can flex your creative muscles with the pricey ones. Side note: just do not buy the super cheap, acrylic yarn. This does not work well for many projects, especially novice ones. Instead, opt for a natural fiber that is simple.

3. Befriend the basics.

Again, keep your distance from the bedazzled choices of yarn. These are not good starter yarns. Instead, buddy up to the basic options. Flex your creative muscle with a bold color choice if you have a hard time accepting the simplicity at this point, but try to keep the color light. The important thing is that you see your stitches as you practice, and a lighter yarn color will make it more apparent when you miss a stitch or make a mistake. Worsted weight wool is one of the most basic options you can go with.

4. Get curious about new ideas.

The beauty of knitting today is that there is a plethora of techniques and options out there for you to experiment with. As you are learning, now is a great time to try out some fun ideas. When you are following a pattern and it throws a challenge at you, give it a shot. Directions for cables and yarns over may scare you at first, but when you get into them, you will find they are not that bad. Plus, did you start knitting for just simple scarves? Probably not! So this is the time to conquer your fear of a decrease and knit those beautiful hats!

5. Search for inspiration and enjoy the creativity.

Scour Pinterest, stalk knitting blogs, browse images of knitted projects to become inspired with what you will knit one day. Think about expanding your repertoire of knitting projects to include headbands, gloves, and other fun "newbie" projects. Many sites will allow you to search their pattern database by skill level so you can find projects that you can complete at this stage and droll over projects that you want to challenge yourself with as you keep practicing. This not only helps you find new projects but when frustration and boredom kick in, you can scroll through your favorite places to reignite the dream you have of becoming a glorious knitter.

6. Use your resources.

There are plenty of resources out there that you can use to get started and to help you advance. This book is one of them! Use it. If you are getting frustrated with something, check out the pages of this book for tips on how to accomplish it or spend a few minutes on YouTube watching a video to nail that purl. You do not need to suffer alone. This and other resources are out there to get you to where you want to be. All else fails? Throw it in a bag and take it into your local yarn shop and get some advice! Maybe join a knitting group in the area so you have a community of knitters to help you learn the tricks of the trade.

7. Put it away before someone (or something) gets hurt!

You have knitted and removed stitches for what feels like hours and are still not past the first row of stitches. You just want to throw it at the TV and cry. Take a deep breath—this has happened (and often still does) to all of us. Put your knitting aside, take a little (or a lot) time to yourself, and then go back at it again when you are ready. If you try to power through the frustration, you will probably contract "crazy knitter fit" and will infect your project with it. You will get so annoyed with the one slipped stitch that you will keep making the same mistake throughout the project, and it almost never ends well. Coming at the problem with calm and rested eyes will often help you solve the problem, at least easier than before, and get you moving again.

8.Know your abbreviations or at least have a cheat sheet handy.

As you progress in your knitting career, you will probably move on to patterns. Many of your patterns will explain the abbreviations they use, but some will not. If you do not have much experience with knitting patterns, it may look like gibberish to you. This is a simple fix: keep a list of abbreviations and a short description of what they are. Add new terms and stitches to the list as you go. Stash this list in your knitting supplies so you can add or reference it as you are working. You will be surprised how this will make your life so much easier.

9. Hold on to your practice projects.

As you are learning, you will have plenty of projects that just do not turn out showcase-worthy. That is normal and actually a good thing. But instead of tossing those practice projects, consider taking them apart to reuse the yarn for another project or using parts of them in a new craft if there are salvageable pieces. Upcycle or recycle these projects later as you become more skilled. Even when you are a knitter either intermediate or advanced, you will have practice projects, and learning this tip now will save you a lot of time and money in the long run.

10. Relax! This is supposed to be fun.

Knitting can be relaxing and fun, or you could let it stress you out and cause anxiety. You should choose knitting for the latter. So what if you mess up? Laugh it off! Knitting takes time and practice, so the more you learn from it, the better you will get. Enjoy the ride. You can take this with you anywhere, you can lose yourself in the repetition, and you can challenge yourself with new ideas. Venture out and try it; you will be surprised at how quickly you will turn from thinking this is too difficult to, "Is this really all it is?!"

How to Pick Your Yarn

Even advanced knitters get flabbergasted with the selection of available yarn. There are just so many beautiful choices! There is always something new. You can fritter away days going through the different options, enjoying the textures and the colors. It can be overwhelming how many choices there are and a challenge picking just the right one for your project. The purpose of this chapter is to help you gather your supplies, so here is where you will learn how to pick your yarn.

As mentioned previously, choosing a basic, worsted wool yarn in a lighter color is excellent to learn on. Choose a medium yarn weight rather than thin or thick. Make sure the texture is smooth. This will be the easiest to learn and practice on. When purchasing from a commercial yarn or craft store, always read the label wrapped around the ball for more important details about the yarn you are considering. You may find that some will indicate that it is better for certain crafts than others.

Reading a yarn label can be a challenge for those that have never looked at one before. Below are some tips on how to decipher the yarn label code:

- *The Largest Letters*—The letters or words dominating the label is the name of the company.
- *Net Weight*—This indicates the bulk of the yarn: light, medium, or bulky. Look for the number "4" on the label. This indicates it is medium. "0" is for lace, "1" and "2" are fine, and "3" is light. "5" and "6" are bulky, and "7" indicates a jumbo weight.

- *Length*—This is the total amount of yarn you will get in a ball. Make sure to check that the length is equal to or more than the project you are planning. If it is not, you will need to pick up more balls.

- *Color and Color Number*—Typically, there is a name given to the color. It can be generic like "Bright Red" or more creative like "Robin Red Breast." There is a more specific color number associated with the color like "A432." If you are purchasing more than one ball of yarn for a project, double check that the color and color name are the same. The color may appear to be similar, but when you start to mix the two balls, you will notice any subtle differences. It is best to do a little check here to avoid a disaster later.

- *Dye Lot*—Similar to checking the color name and number, this Dye Lot number indicates that the yarn was colored in the same batch. Again, this can slightly alter the color of the yarn even if they have the same color name and number. This will be listed as a simple combination of numbers like "567."

- *Fiber Content*—This number and name will be given together. It will appear as a single fiber and percentage, such as "100% wool," or a combination of fibers and percentages, such as "50% acrylic, 50% wool." When beginning for many projects, stick to more natural fibers like wool and avoid acrylic because they will split and slip on your needles. Also, even though cotton is a natural fiber, it does not have much stretch and can be hard for a beginner to work with.

- *Gauge and Laundry Symbols*—Sometimes, the care instructions will be given to you in words and sometimes in images only.

Not all companies provide all this information or in this way, but you will find a lot of it on most commercial yarns. Here is a sample yarn label for you to see some of the information described above:

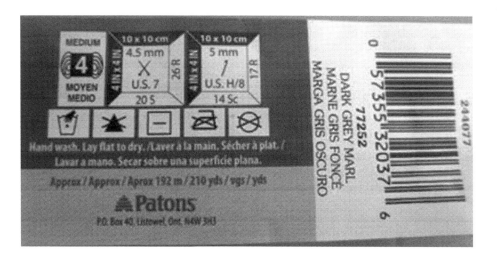

One key symbol provided that is especially important for all knitters, including the advanced ones, is the section with the crossed knitting needles. This is typically a rectangle or square with two knitting needles crossed inside and a lot of numbers and letters placed around it. This little box tells you what knitting gauge and needle size you need. The center where the needles are crossed has a number written above it, for example, "4.5 mm." This is what knitting needle size the company recommends for this yarn. Below this may be another number like "7 US," which indicates the US knitting needle size, in the event, you are shopping and there is no millimeter measurement. To the left of the box are numbers such as "4X4 IN" and on top numbers such as "10X10 CM." This is information about the gauge swatch you need to make. It should be 4 inches wide and 4 inches long or 10 centimeters long and wide. The bottom of the box has a number and letter such as "20 S," and the right of the box has a number and letter such as "26 R." This information is about the stitches and rows. The bottom number and letter tell you that you should get 20 stitches ("S") and 26 rows ("R") into the 4-inch square. If there is another box next to it with a single hook, this is information for crocheting.

Below is an image for you to visually see the label:

It is a good practice to save your yarn label with the swatch you created, so you remember all the information and have the care instructions. If you are giving the project as a gift, include the yarn label so the recipient knows how to care for their new, beautiful present.

If you are not certain about the laundry symbols on the label, below is a cheat sheet to help you decipher the information:

How to Pick Your Needles

You may notice that there are hundreds of different options when it comes to knitting needles. They come in all sorts of sizes and materials. Some people swear by bamboo or wood needles, while others love metal, such as aluminum, ones. Others enjoy the variety and economic benefit of plastic needles. As you continue practicing and trying out different tools, you will develop a preference, just like every knitter.

To begin, select a couple of different needles in different sizes to try out. Do not shy away from the curved, circular needles either. These may end up being your best friend. Circular needles do allow you to knit flat and can actually hold a lot more stitches than flat needles. This is especially handy for large projects. Many knitters love working with wooden needles, especially in the beginning, because of the strength and slight give in the material. They also grip the yarn well, unlike smooth options like some plastics and most metals.

Just as previously suggested to start with medium yarn, start knitting with medium-sized needles. Check for sizes like 6 US, 7 US, or 8 US. If the needles do not have US sizes on them, choose 4 mm, 4.5 mm, or 5 mm. These are best for medium yarns and feel good in your hands. This also applies to the thickness of the needle. Thin needles are great for thinner yarn while thicker needles compliment a thick yarn better. If you have a medium-weight wool yarn, choose a needle with medium thickness.

Another consideration is the needle length. This mainly applies to straight needles, but you will find the needles range in size from 7 inches up to 14 inches. Children typically use the smaller needles, but you may like the shorter sizes in the beginning. Shorter needles can be less difficult to maneuver and easier to use. If a project is large, however, choose a longer needle so it can hold more stitches.

When you choose the pattern you wish to knit and the yarn you will be using to complete the project, choose a needle that corresponds to the pattern instructions and wool label as described above. Do not attempt to knit with a different sized needle than the pattern and wool calls for, especially if you are doing a clothing. This will result in an ill-fitting final project and can be frustrating after all the time and effort you put into it. There is a huge difference between the needle sizes, so make sure it all matches before you begin your project. It takes some attention to the details, but it is worth it in the long run!

Below is a small needle conversion chart to help you when you are purchasing needles so you can quickly determine if the needle will fit your project needs:

Metric/mm	US	Canadian/UK
2	0	14
2.25 OR 2.5	1	13
2.75	2	12
3.0	XX	11
3.25	3	10
3.5	4	XX
3.75	5	9
4.0	6	8
4.5	7	7
5.0	8	6
5.5	9	5
6.0	10	4
6.5	10.5	3
7.0	10.75	2
7.5	XX	1
8.0	11	0

Chapter 2: Basic Knits and Techniques— Including Simple Practice Projects!

Some people say there are several types of knitting stitches; however, there is really only one knit stitch with variations to it. This includes the purl stitch that you probably have heard a bit about already! It really is just a version of a traditional knit stitch. So rest easy, you only have to master one stitch and then have fun learning how to mix it up a little bit. This chapter will illustrate what the basic stitch looks like, along with variations of it, and some simple practice projects you can do to master the different options.

The variations of the basic knit stitch include the following:

• Knitting to the back of a stitch

• Purl

• Purl to the back of a stitch

• Garter

• Stocking

• Reverse

• Ribbing

• Knit one below

Cast On

Before you can even approach these, you must first cast on. Casting in means getting your yarn and needles ready to start knitting. You are creating loops along your needle that will become the initial row of stitching. There are a few methods people use to cast on:

• Single

• Longtail

• Knitted

• Cable

Single and Longtail are great beginners cast on techniques, but you should practice with each method to find what you like the best. Regardless of the method you choose, you need to start with a slipknot. To create these slipknots, follow these simple **Instructions:**

1. Make a loop with your yarn and bring the tail through the loop to create a second loop. This will create a knot at the end. Slide it onto your needle and pull to tighten. That is it!

Now, try out the different cast on methods by following the instructions below:

The Single Cast On

1. Wrap the yarn that is attached to your ball of yarn, called the "working yarn," around your thumb, creating a loop.

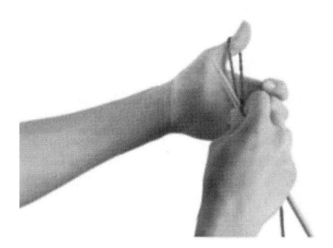

2. Slide your needle under and up through the loop. Remove your thumb and pull the yarn tight.

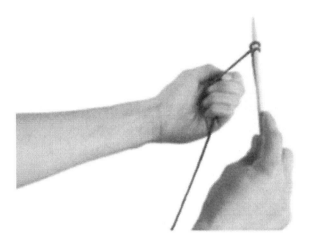

3. Keep repeating the first and second steps until you have the number of loops you need for your project on your needle.

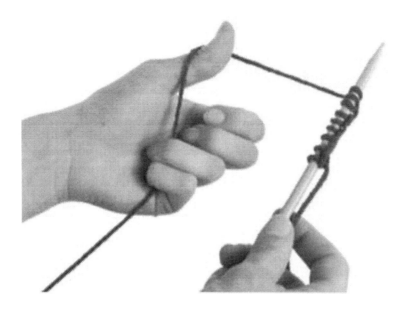

The Longtail Cast On

Before beginning, measure a length of yarn for the tail. For example, if you want to cast on 10 stitches, leave about 12 inches of yarn for the tail. The following instructions are best for right-handed knitters. But you can reverse the directions given for your opposite hand if you are left-handed.

1. In your left hand, place the tail over the top of your pointer finger and thumb. Pinch the tail between your middle and pointer fingers.
2. Pinch the working yarn to your palm of your left hand with your ring and pinky fingers.

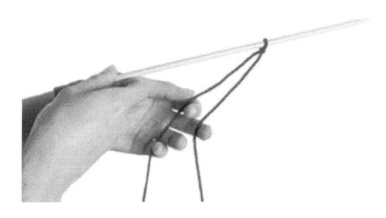

3. In your right hand, hold your needle. Press your needle gently on top of the yarn that is draped between your pointer finger and thumb. Hook the yarn and pull it towards you, creating a loop of yarn around your thumb.

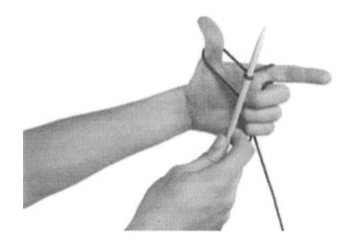

4. Move the needle to the outer piece of the yarn and slide it under your thumb and up out of the loop.

5. Point the needle back to your pointer finger and move it over the yarn connected to your pointer finger and back at your thumb.

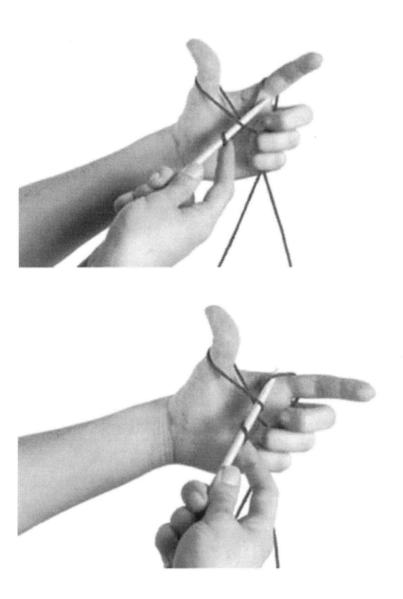

6. Lower the top of your needle back through the loop that is around your thumb.

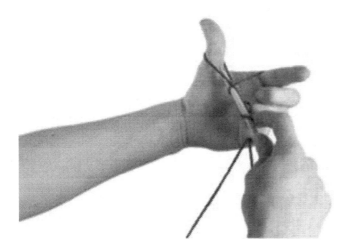

7. Move out your thumb and pull the yarn to tighten.

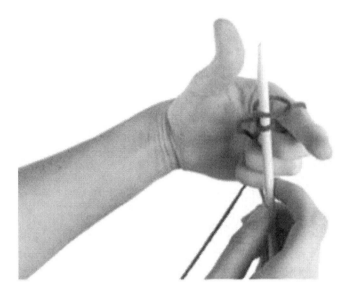

8. Keep repeating Step 6 until you have the number of loops you needed for your project on your needle.

The Knit Cast On

1. The needle with the slip knot is placed in your left hand and the blank needle in your right.

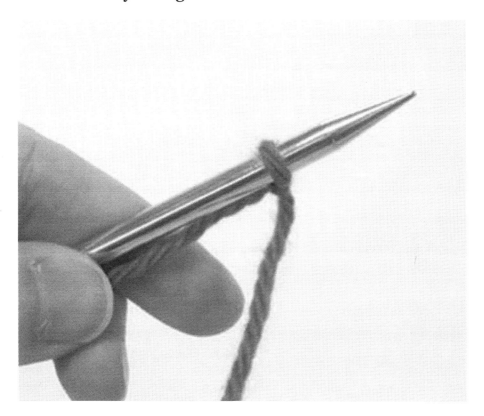

2. Slide the right-hand needle through the loop on the left-hand needle and then bring the right under the left.

3. Using your left hand, twist the working yarn around the left needle. The right needle is moved back inside the loop on the left needle. This creates a loop on the needle in your right hand.

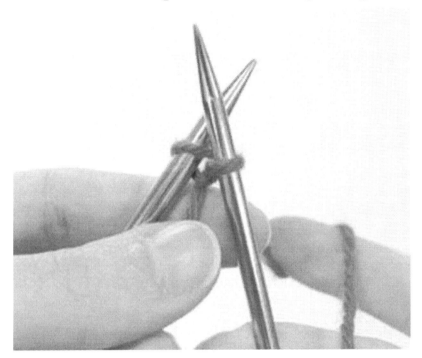

4. Twist the loop on the right needle, slide it onto the left, and remove the right needle.

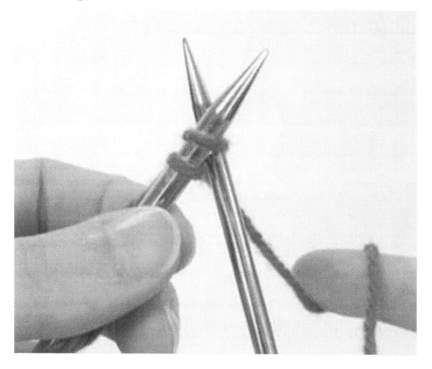

5. Pull the yarn to tighten. This has now created 2 stitches.

6. Keep repeating Steps 2 through 5 until you have the number of loops you needed for your project on your needle.

The Cable Cast On

The beginning is the same as the knit cast on:

1. The needle with the slip knot is placed in your left hand and then the blank needle in your right.

2. Slide the right-hand needle through the loop on the needle in your left hand and bring the right under the left.

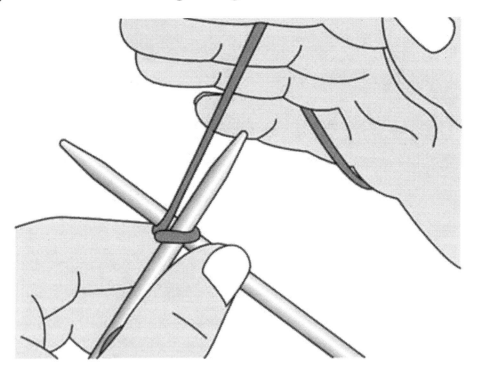

3. Using your left hand, twist the working yarn around the left needle. Move the right needle back inside the loop on the left needle. This creates a loop on the needle in the right hand.

4. Twist the loop on the right needle, slide it onto the left, and remove the right needle.

5. Pull the yarn to tighten. This has now created 2 stitches.

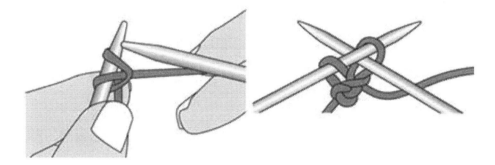

After you create the first two stitches, however, the cable cast on adds a few extra steps:

6. The right-hand needle in your right hand is placed in between the 2 stitches and move it under the left, sliding it through the yarn connecting the 2 stitches.

7. Wrap the working yarn around the tip of the right needle and bring the right needle through the loops. This creates a loop on the needle in your right hand.

8. Twist the loop on the right needle, slide it onto the left, and remove the right needle.

9. Pull the yarn to tighten. This has now created 2 stitches.

10. Keep repeating Steps 2 through 5 until you have the number of loops you needed for your project on your needle.

Basic Knit Stitches

Now that you know how to cast on, you need to learn to knit. To learn the various versions of the knit stitch, begin by practicing the basic knit stitch first.

Basic Knit

1. Place the yarn at the back of the work, and the needle in your right hand is inserted from the left to the right, passing it through the front of the first stitch on the needle in the left.

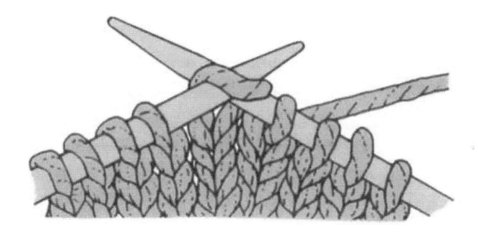

2. Twist the yarn over the right-hand needle.

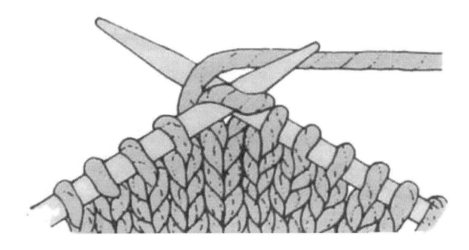

3. A look is created if you pull through and slide the first stitch off the needle in the left hand.

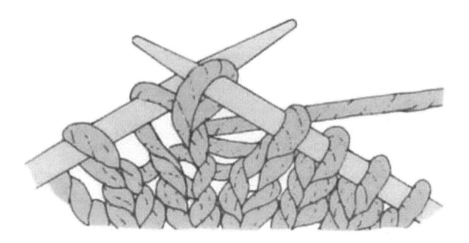

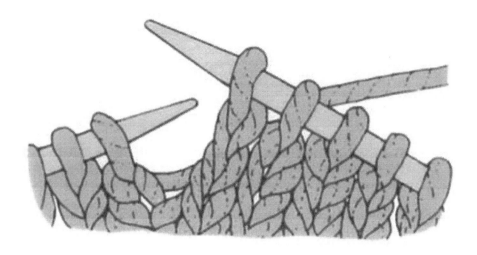

4. Keep repeating Steps 2 and 3 until all the stitches have moved from the left-hand needle to the needle in your right hand.

Knitting to the Back of a Stitch

This variation creates a twisted, ribbed effect and a beautiful texture. To begin:

1. Place the right needle into the back of the stitch on the needle in the left.

The following steps are the same as the basic knit:

2. Twist the yarn over the needle in your right hand.
3. A loop is created when you pull it through and slide the first stitch off the needle in your left hand.
4. Keep repeating Steps 2 and 3 until all the stitches have moved from the needle in your left hand to the needle in the right.

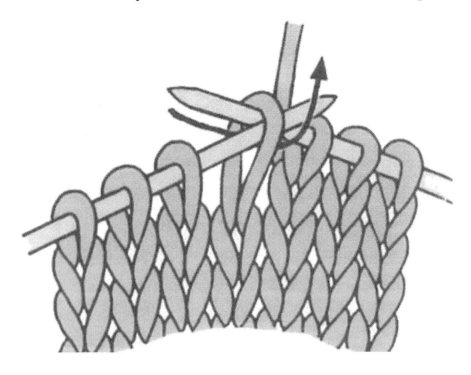

Purl

1. Place the working yarn in the front of the project. The right needle is moved from the right to left through the front of the beginning stitch on the left needle.

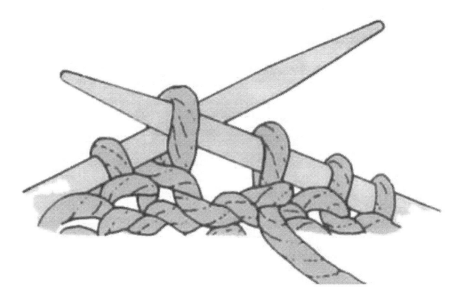

2. Twist the yarn around the right needle.

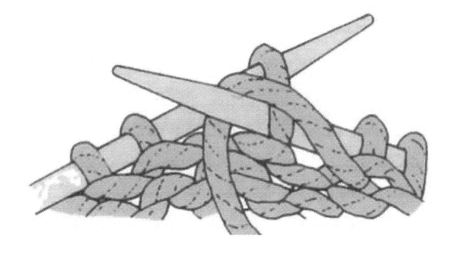

3. Pull through to create a loop and slide the stitch off the left-hand needle.

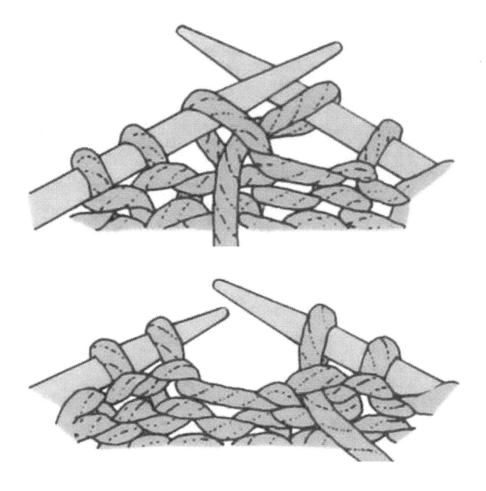

4. Keep repeating Steps 2 and 3 until all the stitches have moved from the left-hand needle to the right-hand needle.

Purl to the Back of a Stitch

To begin:

1. Place the right needle into the back of the stitch on the left needle from the back. Bring the pointed end of the right needle through to the front.

The following steps are the same as the purl:

2. Twist the yarn around the right needle.

3. Pull through to create a loop and slide the stitch off the left-hand needle.

4. Keep repeating Steps 2 and 3 until all the stitches have moved from the left-hand needle to the right-hand needle.

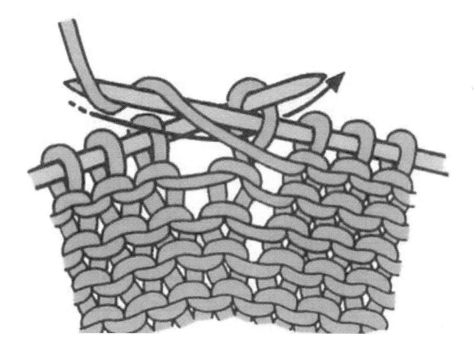

Garter

This is actually a version of working each row the same way. It can be done with each row as a knit or purl row. Typically, the right side is the first row. It is a striking effect, no matter which type of stitch you choose.

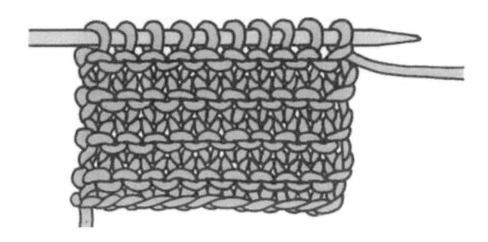

Stocking

This is a variation of the garter stitch. It consists of one full row of knit stitches and the next a full row of purl. It is always started with the knit row on the right side.

Reverse

This is a reverse of the stocking stitch, meaning you start with the row of purl and move to the knit row second. The Purl row is the right side.

Ribbing

Garment edges are typically made from ribbing because of the elastic nature of the knit. There are two most commonly used, the 1X1 and the 2X2. The 1X1 is created by moving from 1 knit stitch to 1 purl stitch on a row. When you alternate 2 knit stitches and then 2 purl stitches on a row, the 2X2 is created. It is important when doing this knit that you knit stitches that were purled on the last row, and the same goes for purling previously knitted stitches.

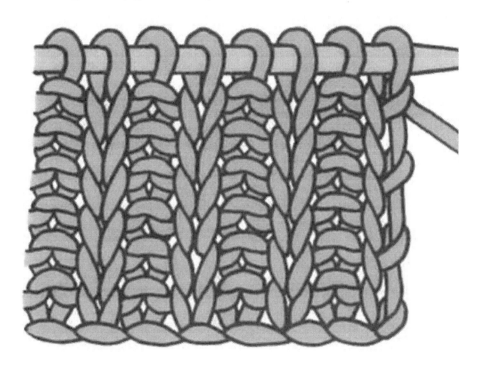

Knit One Below

A thick and sturdy knit is called the "Fisherman's Rib," and it is made up of Knit One Below stitches. To begin:

1. Move the right needle into the following stitch but below the stitch on the left needle. Continue the knitting process as usual.

2. Keep repeating until all the stitches have moved from the needle in your left hand to the needle in your right hand.

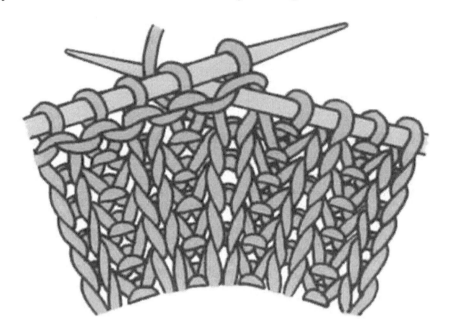

Bind Off

And finally, you now know how to start and knit, but what do you do when you are done? This finish is called "bind off." There are a few different methods you can use to bind off; some of the most common for beginners include the following:

• Standard

• 3-Needle

• Stretchy

Now, try out the different bind off methods by following the instructions below:

Standard

1. With the project's right side facing you, slide the right needle through the first stitch of the work and knit it like a normal stitch.

2. Knit a second stitch normally, then pull the first knitted stitch over the second, and pull the first stitch off the needle. This binds off once stitch.

3. Keep repeating Steps 1 and 2 as needed. When finished and only one stitch remains on the right needle, snip the working yarn and pass it through the last stitch to finish the edge.

3-Needle

For projects that require stability and longevity, this bind off is wonderful. It is also excellent for knits that combine knit and purl stitches because it takes place inside the project, not showing itself on the outside of the finished item. These are common in garment's shoulder seams, along with the top of the hood of a sweater or the joint of a collar.

1. If you are using two needles, have your stitches on both needles. If you are using a circular needle, have your stitches on either end of the needle. Place the inside or the "wrong side" of the pieces together.

2. Taking the third needle, knit through the first stitch on each
   needle and twist the yarn to knit the 2 stitches to one another.
   Drop the stitches from each of the parallel needles, leaving 1
   stitch on the third needle.

3. Do the same thing for the second stitch on the parallel needles leaving the second stitch on the third needle. Using one of the parallel needles, move the first stitch on top of the second and drop it off the needle, similar to a regular knit bind off. This creates one bound off stitch.

4. Keep repeating Steps 1 through 3 until all the stitches are bound. As this illustrates, it is important to have an equal number of stitches on each needle prior to starting.

Stretchy

Items that need to fit snuggly around something, like a mug or the body, benefit from a stretchy bind off. You can find this type of bind off around a neckline or the toes of socks or in fun projects, like a mug cozy.

There are many versions of a stretchy finish; however, the most common is the "Knit 2 Together Through the Back Loop."

1. On the left needle, knit the first two stitches onto the right.

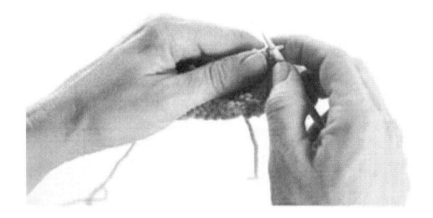

2. Slide the left needles inside the front of both stitches and knit together, creating a bound stitch.

49

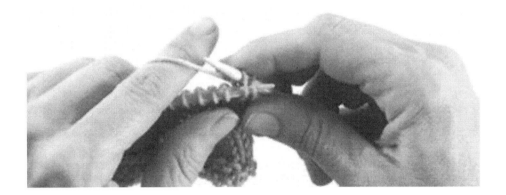

3. Knit the next stitch from the left to the right and slide the left needle into the front of the two stitches. Together, knit them through the back loop.

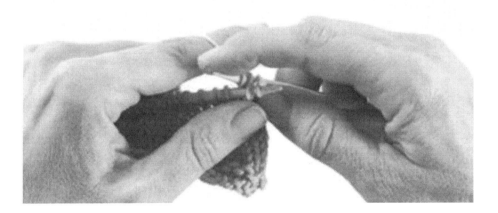

4. Keep repeating the third step until only one stitch remains on the right needle. Tie this off as you would a standard bind off.

Practice Project

Before you begin a project, make sure to create a practice swatch of the knit first, using the yarn you have chosen. This quick little test will make sure you are confident tackling the project you have chosen using the needles and yarn you have selected. If you do not have luck with your swatch, swap out the yarn and needles until you have the desired effect you are looking for. If you are just beginning using a medium weight wool and medium needle in a shorter length, create swatches of each of the above-listed knits using a different cast on methods. Once you are done with those swatches, it is time to tackle a few for your first, real knitting projects! How exciting!

Below are a few simple beginner's projects that will help you get more comfortable with repeating stitches. If you feel that the swatches were enough of an exercise, go ahead and move on to the next chapter. If you are wanting more practice but on a larger scale, check out these projects below.

The Garter Stitch Scarf

To start this project, grab a set of knitting needles and a ball or two of yarn and cast on. Keep knitting back and forth with garter stitches and bind off when you are done. If you want to try another version, consider changing up the stitch to a basic knit or purl. Follow the same basic instructions and create a couple more simple scarves.

Choosing a practice project like this allows you to try out your cast on and bind off skills, as well as perfect your knitting technique for some of the more basic knits.

The Stocking Knit Washcloth

An added practice project is the sticking knit washcloth. This can be an intimidating project. Do not worry if it starts to curl as you work, this is normal!

Here is a more detailed pattern and Instructions:

Supplies:

- 1 100% cotton yarn, 2.5 ounces skein
- 7 US knitting needle pair
- Scissors

Gauge and size:

Gauge—20 S (stitches) and 27 R (rows) per 4 inches. Not critical, but keep as close as possible. Tighter washcloths are preferred over looser knits, so try to keep it close to this gauge. *Size*—12 ¼-inch wide x 11-inch long.

Instructions:

1. Cast on 61 stitches.
2. *Row 1*—Knit completely across the front side.
3. *Row 2*—Use a 1 x 1 rib knit, knit one stitch, and purl the next across the entire row.
4. Keep repeating Steps 2 and 3 until your yarn is almost gone. Bind off.
5. For the excess yarn, trim it away and weave in the loose ends. You are done!

Wrap Made of Ribbing

This is a more advanced practice project mainly because it again challenges you to switch from knitting to purling throughout the whole process. For this reason, it is advisable to complete a washcloth or two before moving on to this project, unless you feel confident after your practice swatches.

This project is another simple pattern, and you can choose how big you want to make it. That being said, making it functional means making it about 30 inches by 34 inches. This size means you will need about 3 balls of 5-ounce yarn and you can choose a medium weight, although this is gorgeous in a lighter wool. Choosing a "3" instead of a "4" can really highlight your stitching and make a soft wrap you can enjoy over and over again.

As you begin your project, cast on and start with a 2 x 2 rib knit, knitting 2 stitches and purling 2 stitches across until you reach your desired width. Move to the next row and make sure your knit and purl stitches line up appropriately. When you reach your desired length, bind off and enjoy. It will be a challenge to get going at first, but after a couple of rows, you will find yourself flowing through to the end like a champion!

Chapter 3: Beginner Knitting Projects—Start to Finish

Now that you have learned the basics of knitting, it is time to really tackle some fun projects. Even as a novice knitter, you can create gorgeous gifts for friends and family or something beautiful for yourself. There is a whole wide world of patterns and ideas out there, but it is important that you pick a few beginner projects that you can both feasibly accomplish and be proud of at the end. This chapter is stuffed full of different patterns and ideas so that no matter what you want to make, you will probably find a pattern for it here.

In this chapter, you will find patterns for the following:

- Hats
- Scarves
- Afghans
- Cushion cover
- Slippers
- Legwarmers
- Skirt
- Wreath

Enjoy browsing the different tutorials, choose one to try out, get your needles and yarn ready, and go have some fun! Enjoy your first real knitting project!

Hats

Hats are a wonderful place to start flexing your knitting talent. Once you complete one or two of the practice projects in the previous chapter, you should be ready to take on this challenge. It is a little more challenging than a flat project because you are going to want to use circular needles (but some of the patterns below still use straight!) and create a three-dimensional project, but it is not out of your reach as a newbie.

Basic Beanie

Supplies:

Needles—US 9 or 5.5 mm
Yan Weight—4, medium weight, about 100 yards
Extra—yarn needle for sewing closed

Gauge:

Gauge—16-20 S (stitches) in 4 inches

Instructions:

1. Cast on 74 stitches.

2. Knit a 1 x 1 ribbed knit, knit one, and purl one for 6 rows.

3. Move to a stocking stitch, knitting one full row and then purling one full row until the total length is 7 inches, or 18 centimeters, from the casted edge to the end that is a purled row.

4. On the following row, knit two together across for 37 stitches.

5. Purl one full row.

6. Knit two together across a full row ending in 1 knit stitch for 19 stitches.

7. Cut 12 inches, or 30 centimeters, of yarn and thread it through a yarn needle.

8. Gently pull the final row of stitching from the needle and move the yarn needle through each stitch, pulling slightly to tighten and then whipstitch the seam together.

9. Add a flourish on the top, like a pom-pom or a flower to the side, if you want. You did it!

Cobblestone Hat

Supplies:

Needles—US 7
Yarn—4, medium weight, about 100 yards or more

Gauge:

Gauge—about 25 S in 4 inches

Instructions:

1. Cast on 86 stitches.

2. First 10 rows—Knit garter stitches.

3. Row 11 and each odd row—Knit one full row.

4. Rows 12, 20, 22, 24, 32, and 34—Purl one full row.

5. Rows 14, 16, and 18—Knit 1, purl 3, knit 6, purl 3, repeat the purl 3, knit 6, and purl 3 until the last stitch, and knit 1 final stitch.

6. Rows 26, 28, and 30—knit 1, purl 6, knit 6, repeat the purl 6 and knit 6 until the last stitch, and knit 1 final stitch.

7. Begin to decrease the crown:

   a. Row 35—Knit 1, knit 5, SSK (slip, slip, knit), repeat the knit 5 and SSK until the last stitch, and knit 1 final stitch for 74 stitches.

   b. Row 36 and each even row—Purl one full row.

   c. Row 37—Knit 1, knit 4, SSK, repeat the knit 4 and SSK until the last stitch, and knit 1 final stitch for 62 stitches.

   d. Row 39—Knit 1, knit 3, SSK, repeat the knit 3 and SSK until the last stitch, and knit 1 final stitch for 50 stitches.

   e. Row 41—Knit 1, knit 2, SSK, repeat the knit 2 and SSK until the last stitch, and knit 1 final stitch for 38 stitches.

   f. Row 43—Knit 1, knit 1, SSK, repeat the knit 1 and SSK until the last stitch, and knit 1 final stitch for 26 stitches.

   g. Row 45—Knit 1, SSK to the last stitch, and knit 1 final stitch for 14 stitches.

8. Leave a long tail from your working yarn and cut the ball off.

9. Using a yarn needle, if necessary, bring the tail through the remaining stitches on your needle. Pull closed and sew the seam together. Interlace the ends of the project and enjoy your stylish new cap!

SSK or Slip, Slip, Knit **Instructions:

1. The first stitch is slid on the left needle to the right, like you would do when knitting, but do not knit it. Slide the second stitch from the left to the right.

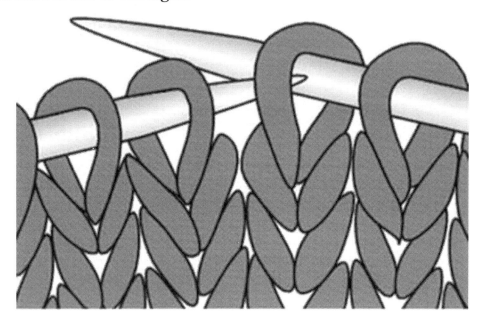

2. The left needle is moved into the front loops of the two stitches you just moved to the right needle.

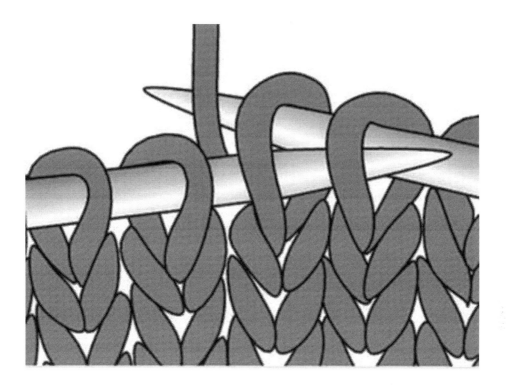

3. Twist the yarn as you normally do when knitting around the right needle and knit the 2 "slipped" stitches together.

Hoodie Hat

Supplies:

Needles—US 17
Yarn—4, medium weight, about 50 total grams, 4 strands
Extra—yarn needle, fun **Yarn**—about 10 yards

Gauge:

- 16 S in 4 inches, not required but advisable

Instructions:

1. With the 4 strands, cast on 22 stitches.

2. Knit each row until you make a 24-inch wide rectangle.

3. Cast off with 15 inches of a yarn tail.

4. Fold your rectangle in half and sew the back seam together with the yarn needle. Turn the hat right-side out so that the seam is on the inside.

5. Add fun yarn to the two sides of the hat so that it hangs down by the ears in tassels and one long tassel at the top, if you want.

To make a tassel:

1. With fun yarn, wrap it around your 4 fingers approximately 20 times. Tie securely through the loop.

2. Tie a second piece of yarn towards the top of the bundle where it is tied together so there is a small ball formed at the top.

3. Trim the ends of the tassel so they are loose.

4. Insert the ends of the tie holding the bundle together at the sides and on the top of your hat and tie securely on the inside. Intertwine the ends into the finished work.

Scarves

The previous chapter gave some basic instructions on how to complete a simple scarf using basic knits. This section will give you a variation of how to make a different style of scarf that is still a beginner level but fun!

Slanted Ridge Cowl or Infinity Scarf

Supplies:

> ***Needles*—**US 35 or 19 mm
> ***Yarn*—**6, Bulky weight, about 5 balls

Gauge and size:

> ***Gauge*—**4 S X 9 R for 4 inches in a garter stitch

Size—About 26 inches around x 15-inch wide

Instructions:

1. Cast on 26 stitches.

2. Row 1—On the wrong side, increase the first stitch by knitting into the front and then back to the next stitch. Repeat the last 2 stitches, knitting the last 2 together.

3. Row 2—Knit the entire row.

4. Repeat Step 3 until the side measurement is about 26 inches, and it ends on the right side row.

5. Bind off knitwise.

6. Sew the cast on and bind off edges together to make the cowl or infinity scarf.

Garden Trellis Scarf

Supplies:

Needles—US 5

Yarn—6, bulky, 4 balls or skeins

Gauge and size:

Gauge—24 S for 4 inches in Stocking Stitch
Size—8-inch wide x 62-inch long

Instructions:

1. Cast on 49 stitches.

2. Row 1—On the wrong side, slip 1, purl 1, knit 1, purl until the last 3 stitches, then knit 1, and purl 2 final stitches.

3. Row 2—On the right side, slip 1 with the yarn on the back, knit 1, purl 1, knit 1, and slip 5. Repeat the knit 1 and skip 5 until the final 4 stitches, then knit 1, purl 1, and knit 2.

4. Row 3 and each odd row—Repeat Row 1 or Step 2 instructions.

5. Row 4—Slip 1 with the yarn on the back, knit 1, purl 1, knit 3, knit 1 under the loose strand, and knit 2. Repeat the knit 3 and knit 1 under the loose strand and knit 2 until the last 4 stitches. Then knit 1, purl 1, and knit 2.

6. Row 6—Slip 1 with the yarn on the back, knit 1, purl 1, slip 3, knit 1, and slip 5. Repeat the knit 1 and slip 5 until the last 7 stitches. Then knit 1, slip 3, purl 1, and knit 2.

7. Row 8—Slip 1 with the yarn on the back, knit 1, purl 1, knit 1 under the loose strand, and knit 5. Repeat the knit 1 under the loose strand and knit 5 until the last 4 stitches. Then knit 1 under the loose strand, purl 1, and knit 2.

8. Repeat Steps 2 through 7 until the total length is about 59 or 60 inches, or just a few inches short of the total length.

9. Repeat Row 1 instructions.

10. Bind off knitwise and intertwine the ends into the project.

Knit 1 Under the Loose Strand **Instructions:

1. Place the right needle beneath the loose stand and insert it into the next stitch knitwise, going from front to the back. Knit the stitch as usual.

2. Move the new stitch from underneath the strand.

Afghans

Creating gorgeous knit blankets and throws are a perfect gift for someone or accent to your home. In addition, many people hold on to knitted afghans for generations, making them the perfect gift for a wedding or shower. In the previous chapter, you learned how to make a traditional afghan, but in this chapter, you will take the same concept and add a modern twist or two to get a little more creative with these beginner patterns. Have fun!

Cushy Throw

Supplies:

Needles—US 7, jumbo, circular recommended
Yarn—7, jumbo, 8 balls or skeins **Extra**—
yarn needle

Gauge and size:

Gauge—3 stitches in 4 inches, 4.5 rows in 4 inches with a stocking stitch; make sure to follow this gauge and use a needle to achieve this gauge.
Size—40-inch wide x 50-inch long

Instructions:

1. Cast on 30 stitches.

2. Knit 4 rows.

3. Row 5—On the wrong side, knit 3 and then purl until the last 3 stitches. Knit the final 3 stitches.

4. Row 6—Knit the entire row.

5. Repeat Steps 3 and 4 until the total length is approximately 47 inches long and is a wrong-side row.

6. Knit 4 rows.

7. Bind off knitwise and weave in the ends into the project.

Effortless Afghan

Supplies:

Needles—US 11 or 8 mm, circular recommended
Yarn—6, bulky, 4 balls or skeins

Gauge and size:

Gauge—8 S X 13 R in 4 inches in stocking stitch
Size—52-inch wide x 59-inch long

Instructions:

1. Cast on 104 stitches. Do **not** join.

2. Knit 3 rows with a garter stitch, starting on the wrong side.

3. Begin the pattern called "Crystal Lace":

   a. Row 1—On the right side, knit 7, knit 2 together, and knit 9. Repeat the knit 2 together, knit 9 seven times, then knit 2 together, and finally knit 7.

   b. Row 2 and all even rows—Knit 2, then purl until the last 2 stitches, and then knit 2.

   c. Row 3—Knit 6, knit 2 together 2 times, and knit 7. Repeat the knit 2 together two times, knit 7 seven times, then knit 2 together 2 times, and finally knit 6.

   d. Row 5—Knit 5, knit 2 together 3 times, and knit 5. Repeat the knit 2 together 3 times, knit 5 seven times, then knit 2 together 3 times, and finally knit 5.

   e. Row 7—Knit 4, knit 2 together 4 times, and knit 3. Repeat the knit 2 together 4 times, knit 3 seven times, then knit 2 together 4 times, and finally knit 4.

   f. Row 9—Knit 3, knit together 5 times, and knit 1. Repeat the knit together 5 times, knit 1 seven times, then knit 2 together 5 times, and finally knit 3.

   g. Row 11—Repeat Step "e" or the seventh row.

   h. Row 13—Repeat Step "d" or the fifth row.

i. Row 15—Repeat Step "c" or the third row.

j. Row 17—Repeat Step "b" or the second row.

k. Continue the pattern until the afghan measures about 57 inches long, stopping on the 17th row of the pattern.

4. Use a garter stitch to knit 3 rows.

5. Bind off knitwise on the wrong side and weave the ends into the project.

** Knit 2 together **Instructions:**

1. **Working from the front to the back, bring your right hand needle and move it through 2 of the stitches at one time.**

1) insert RH needle through two stitches

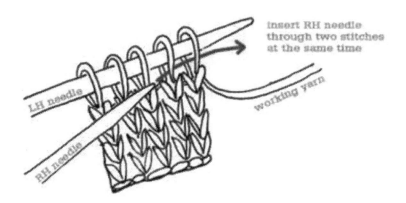

2. Take the working yarn and twist it around the tip of the right hand needle, like when knitting a regular stitch. Using the tip of the right hand needle ,bring the loop around the back and insert through the 2 stitches to bring it to the front.

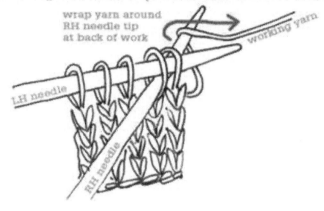

2) wrap yarn around RH needle tip, then
   pull up a stitch (same as a knit stitch)

3. **Knit a stitch on the right hand needle. Allow the two** stitches **knitted together to "fall" off the left hand needle.**

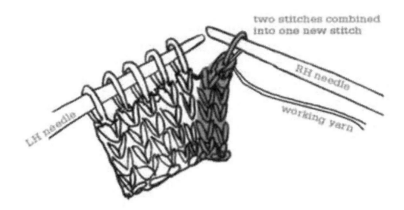

3) drop original stitches off needles

two stitches combined into one new stitch

RH needle

working yarn

LH needle

Cushion Cover

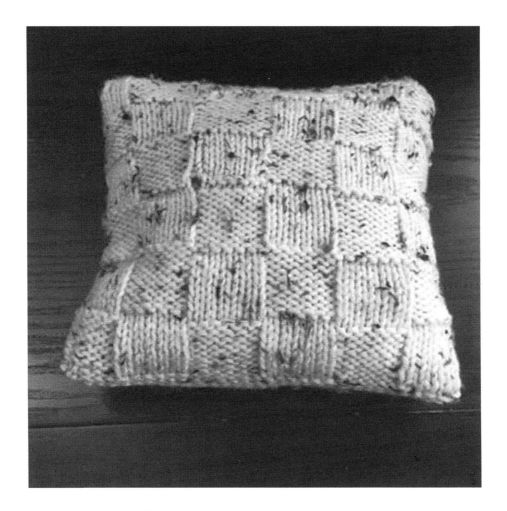

Creating a custom pillow or cushion cover is a great way to change up the look and feel of the room and showcase your skills. With the wide selection of colors, you can create the perfect match for any room.

Supplies:

Needles—US 17
Yarn—4, medium weight, about 50 total grams, 4 strands
Extra—yarn needle

Gauge:

16 S in 4 inches

Instructions:

1. Cast on 36 stitches.

2. For rows 1 to 42—Knit a full row.

3. Row 43 to 50—Knit 7, purl 6, knit 6, purl 6, knit 6, purl 6, and knit 1.

4. Row 51 to 58—Knit 1, purl 6, knit 6, purl 6, knit 6, purl 6, and knit 7.

5. Repeat Steps 3 and 4 two more times to create a 6-by-6 basket weave pattern.

6. For the final 16 rows—Knit a full row.

7. Bind off knitwise.

8. Fold the rectangle in half and, using the yarn needle, sew the sides together to create the square cushion cover. Close the cover with a decorative button, if desired.

Slippers

If you or someone you know always has chilly toes, whip up a pair of these and you will have some thankful, warm toes!

Supplies:

Needles—US 10.5 or 6.5 mm **Yarn**—
6, super bulky, 2 balls or skeins
Extra—yarn needle

Instructions:

1. Cast on 46 stitches.

2. Rows 1 through 12—Complete each row with garter stitches.

3. On row 13—Bind off 18 stitches at the beginning. Finish the row.

4. On row 14—Bind off 18 stitches at the beginning, leaving 10 stitches in the middle.

5. For the remaining stitches, continue the garter stitch of an additional 8 ¾ inches.

6. Bind off and leave a yarn tail about 12 inches long. Your knitting will appear like the letter "T."

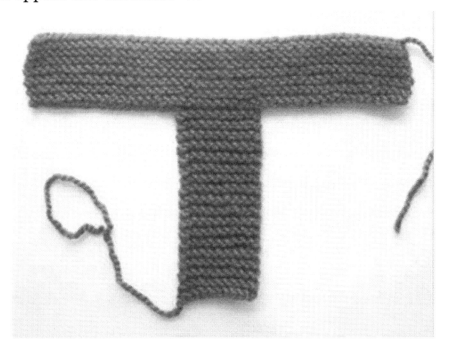

7. Construct the slippers:

   a. Fold one part of "T" on top of the toe or the bottom of the "T."

b. Fold the second part of the "T" on top of the first and the toe, making 3 layers.

c. With your yarn needle, stitch the 3 toe layers together and the two open sides, leaving the folded top part open.

d. Trim tail, weave loose ends into the project, and turn right side out.

8. Repeat for the second slipper.

**Size up for Medium to Large shoe sizes:

- Cast on—50 stitches.
- Row 13—Bind off at 20 stitches.

- Row 14—Bind off at 20 stitches.

- For remaining stitching—garter stitch until the piece measures 9 ¼ inches.

Leg Warmers

For the stylish friend or family member (or for yourself!), these chunky, warm leg warmers are a perfect fall or winter accessory. Thankfully, they are simple to make and a great way to take pride in your new skill set each time you slip them on.

Supplies:

Needles—US 11 or 8 mm, 12-inch circular needles recommended.
Yarn—8, super bulky, 180 yards or about 2 balls
Extra—Stitch marker

Instructions:

1. Cast on 34 stitches and join in the round.

2. Until the knitting is 2.5 inches long—repeat knit 1 and purl 1.

3. Use the basic knit stitch for the following rows until the project is 13 inches long.

4. Add another 2.5 inches by repeating knit 1 and purl 1.

5. Bind off and intertwine the ends into the project.

6. Repeat the process for the second leg warmer.

7. Consider adding a button, decorative yarn or ribbon, or other embellishments to the "top" of the leg warmer, if you desire.

**Join in the Round Instructions:

1. Slip the last stitch (or the first stitch that was cast on) off the left needle onto the right needle.

2. Lift the second stitch on the right needle (or the last stitch that was cast on) over the first stitch and on the left needle.

3. Pull tight, place the stitch marker on the right needle or hooked into a stitch to indicate where the row ends, and continue knitting with the left needle stitches.

Newborn Skirt

When a new baby is born, it is the perfect time to give something useful, meaningful, and generational to the mother-to-be and new bundle of joy. Knitting a simple newborn skirt means the baby can look stylish, the mother can feel appreciated as a valued friend or family member of yours, and it can be saved for future generations to wear. It is that special, and that easy!

Supplies:

Needles—US 10 or 6mm, US 11 or 8 mm, knitting needles (circular or double-pointed)
Yarn—5, bulky, 1-2 balls or skeins
Extra—Stitch marker

Gauge and size:

Gauge—3 S X 4 R in 1 inch using a stocking stitch
Size—13-inch waist circumference, 16-inch hem circumference, 6.5-inch height

Instructions:

1. Using the US 10 needles or circular needle, cast on 48 stitches and join in the round.

2. Rows 1 through 6—Knit 2, purl 2, and repeat for the entire row.

3. Rows 7 through 26—Change to US 11 needles or circular needle and knit around each row.

4. Bind off and intertwine the ends into the project.

Wreath

When you move into a new home or want to give a special housewarming or hostess gift, consider this fun and easy wreath! It will be unexpected and memorable, just what you want to accomplish when welcoming someone to their new home or thanking them for having you over. It can also let your neighbors know about your new, amazing hobby.

Supplies:

Needles—US 8
Yarn—4, medium, 2 balls or skeins
Extra—yarn needle, 12-inch diameter foam wreath form, straight pins

Gauge:

Gauge—4 S X 6 R for 1 inch

Instructions:

1. Cast on 28 stitches.

2. Row 1 and all odd rows—Knit one full row.

3. Row 2 and all even rows—Purl one full row.

4. Repeat this stocking stitch until the length is 37 inches.

5. Bind off and leave a yarn tail 16 inches long.

6. Attach the top of the scarf to the wreath form with a pin and smooth the scarf around the form, pinning along the way to keep it in place.

7. After pinning the scarf to the form using the yarn needle, sew the top to the bottom and create a circle. Whip stitch the open edges closed on the backside of the wreath form. Remove the pins.

8. Add embellishments to the wreath, such as letters or flowers, as desired.

Chapter 4: Combination Beginner Knit Projects

How did you do on the beginner projects from Chapter 3? Did you have fun trying out some new techniques? Were you surprised at how creative you can be with just the basic knitting skills?

It is incredible how much you can do with just a few skills you have practiced. Now, it's time to add a few more techniques together. The following projects in this chapter are still considered beginner projects, but they combine a few more techniques together to push your skill set more. It could be said that some of the techniques added to these projects are more "intermediate" but the overall project is beginner level.

A few of the fun projects you can get into through this chapter include children's ponchos, vests, socks, and coffee coozies, to name a few. Now, get your needles out and some skeins of yarn and find your next project to start on!

Ponchos and Vets

These variations of a scarf make it appear like you are a master knitter but, again, only make you push your skill set a little bit to accomplish such a beautiful result. Enjoy making a present for a little one, or for yourself, and give gifts that matter.

Child's Poncho

Supplies:

Needles—US 8 or 5 mm
Yarn—5, bulky, up to 3 balls or skeins
Extra—Yarn needle

Gauge and size:

Gauge—15 S X 22 R in 4 inches with a stocking stitch
Size—Up to 26.5 inches across chest X up to 17.5 inches long

Instructions (for 12 months' size):

1. Cast on 65 stitches.

2. Row 1—One the wrong side, knit 1, purl 1, and knit 1. Repeat the purl 1 and knit 1 until the end of the row.

3. Row 2—On the right side, knit 1, knit 2 together, and repeat until the last 4 stitches. Slip 1, knit 1, pass the slipped stitch over, and finally knit 2.

4. Row 3—Purl the entire row.

5. Rows 4 to 6—Knit with a stocking stitch.

6. Repeat Steps 4 and 5 ten times for 43 stitches.

7. On the next row, on the right side, knit 2, knit 2 together, and knit until the last 4 stitches. Slip 1, knit 1, pass the slipped stitch over, and finally knit 2.

8. Complete 1 row of purl stitches.

9. Repeat the last two rows 5 times for 31 stitches.

10. Bind off knitwise.

11. Repeat for a second piece. Attach the center and back seams with the yarn needle, trim ends, and weave into the project.

**Adjust for Larger Sizes:

Size 18 Months—

- Cast on 73 stitches.
- Step 6—Repeat 10 times for 51 stitches.
- Step 9—Repeat 9 times for 31 stitches.

Size 2/4—

- Cast on 85 stitches.
- Step 6—Repeat 10 times for 63 stitches.
- Step 9—Repeat 14 times for 33 stitches.

Size 6/8—

- Cast on 97 stitches.
- Step 6—Repeat 10 times for 75 stitches.
- Step 9—Repeat 19 times for 35 stitches.

Adult Two-Piece Poncho

Supplies:

> **Needles**—US 8 or 5 mm
> **Yarn**—5, bulky, 3 balls or skeins

Gauge and size:

Gauge—15 S X 22 R for 4 inches in a stocking stitch

Size—20.5 inches

Instructions for Size Small:

1. Cast on 55 stitches.

2. Rows 1 to 3—Knit the full row.

3. Row 4—On the right side, knit the full row.

4. Row 5—Knit 3, purl until the last 3 stitches, and finish with 3 knit stitches.

5. Repeat Steps 3 and 4 until the project is 29 inches and ends in a wrong side faced for the next row.

6. Knit two more full rows.

7. Bind off knitwise.

8. Repeat for a second piece. Attach the short end of the first piece to the end of the long end of the second piece with the yarn needle. Repeat for the short end of the second piece to the opposite end of the long side of the first piece.

Diagram

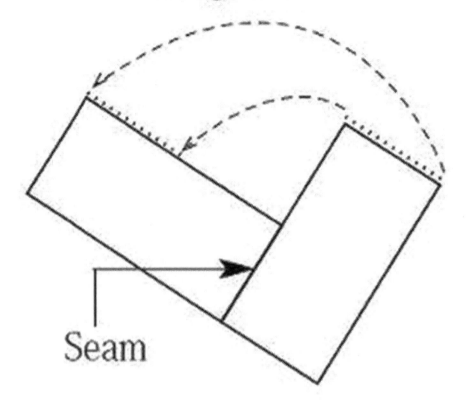

Seam

**Adjust for Larger Sizes:

Size Large—

- Cast on 60 stitches.
- Step 5—Repeat until the project is 32 inches.

Size 3 XL—

- Cast on 65 stitches.
- Step 5—Repeat until the project is 34 inches.

Tie-Front Vest

Supplies:

Needles—US 10.5 or 6.5 mm
Yarn—5, bulky, 4 balls or skeins
Extra—2 stitch holders, yarn needle

Gauge and size:

Gauge—14 S X 18 R in 4 inches using a stocking stitch
Size—28 inches

Instructions for Size Small:

1. Create the Back—

   a. Cast on 63 stitches.

   b. Row 1—On the right side, purl 1, knit 1, repeat 4 times, and then knit 6. Repeat this pattern 4 times, then purl 1, knit 1, and repeat 3 times, ending in 1 purl stitch.

   c. Row 2—Knit 1, purl 1, repeat 4 times and then purl 6. Repeat this pattern 4 times, then knit 1, purl 1, and repeat 3 times, ending in 1 knit stitch.

   d. Repeat Steps 2 and 3 until the project is 20 inches and ends with row 2.

2. Create the Shoulder Shape—

   a. Bind off 8 stitches and begin the following 4 rows, keeping the 31 stitches that remain on a stitch holder.

3. Create the Left Front—

   a. Cast on 32 stitches.

   b. Row 1—On the right side, knit 6. After that, knit 1, purl 1, and repeat 4 times. Repeat the whole set 2 times. End with knit 1 and purl 1 repeated for 2 times.

   c. Row 2—Knit 1 and purl 1 for 2 times. Knit 1, purl 1 four times, and then purl 6. Repeat the whole set of knit 1, purl 1 four times, and then purl 6 for 2 more times.

d. Repeat Steps "b" and "c" until the project is 20 inches and ends with row 2.

4. Create the Shoulder Shape—

   a. Bind off 8 stitches, begin the next, and follow with the alternate row, keeping the 16 stitches that remain on a stitch holder.

5. Create the Right Front—

   a. Cast on 32 stitches.

   b. Row 1—On the right side, purl 1, knit 1, and repeat 2 times. Purl 1, knit 1 four times, and then knit 6. Repeat the whole set of purl 1 and knit 1 four times, and then knit 6 for 2 more times.

   c. Row 2—Purl 6. After, purl 1, knit 1, and repeat this 4 times. Repeat this whole set 2 times. Then purl 1, knit 1, and repeat 2 times.

   d. Repeat Steps "b" and "c" until the project is 20 inches and ends with row 1.

6. Create the collar—

   a. Sew shoulder seams together.

   b. Place right sides together and work-in purl 1, knit 1 ribbing along the 16 stitches from the right front stitching holder, 31 stitches from the backstitching holder, and 16 stitches from the left front stitching holder. 63 total stitches.

   c. Continue ribbing for 7 inches. Bind off ribbing.

   d. Insert markers on the edges of the back and front sides 8 inches below the shoulder seam.

   e. Sew the side seams from the casted edge to the markers using the yarn needle.

7. Create the ties—

   a. Cast on 60 stitches.

   b. Bind off.

   c. Repeat a second time.

   d. Attach the ties to the edges of the front in the middle, if desired.

**Adjust for Larger Size:

Size Medium:

- Supplies—**Yarn**—5 balls or skeins.
- Cast on (Back)—77 stitches.
- Row 1 (Back)—Repeat 5 times.
- Row 2 (Back)—Repeat 5 times.
- Shoulder Shape—Bind off 10 stitches and leave 37 stitches for stitch holder.
- Cast on (Left Front)—36 stitches.
- Row 1 (L Front)—Repeat 2 times and then 4 times.
- Row 2 (L Front)—Repeat 4 times and then 2 times.
- Should Shape—Bind off 10 stitches and leave 16 stitches for stitch holder.
- Cast on (Right Front)—36 stitches.
- Row 1 (R Front)—Repeat 2 times and then 4 times.
- Row 2 (R Front)—Repeat 4 times and then 2 times.
- Collar, Step "b"—Rib stitch 16 stitches, 37 stitches from back stitching holder, and 16 stitches from the left front stitching

holder. 69 total stitches.

- Collar, Step "d"—9 inches below.

Size Large:

- Supplies—**Yarn**—6 balls or skeins.
- Cast on (Back)—91 stitches.
- Row 1 (Back)—Repeat 6 times.
- Row 2 (Back)—Repeat 6 times.
- Shoulder Shape—Bind off 13 stitches and leave 39 stitches for stitch holder.
- Cast on (Left Front)—44 stitches.
- Row 1 (L Front)—Repeat 3 times and then 1 time.
- Row 2 (L Front)—Repeat 1 time and then 3 times.
- Should Shape—Bind off 13 stitches and leave 18 stitches for stitch holder.
- Cast on (Right Front)—44 stitches.
- Row 1 (R Front)—Repeat 3 times and then 1 time.
- Row 2 (R Front)—Repeat 1 time and then 3 times.
- Collar, Step "b"—Rib stitch 18 stitches, 39 stitches from back stitching holder, and 18 stitches from the left front stitching holder. 75 total stitches.
- Collar, Step "d"—10 inches below.

Size XL:

- Supplies—**Yarn**—7 balls or skeins.
- Cast on (Back)—105 stitches.

- Row 1 (Back)—Repeat 7 times.
- Row 2 (Back)—Repeat 7 times.
- Shoulder Shape—Bind off 16 stitches and leave 41 stitches for stitch holder.
- Cast on (Left Front)—50 stitches.
- Row 1 (L Front)—Repeat 3 times and then 4 times.
- Row 2 (L Front)—Repeat 4 times and then 3 times.
- Should Shape—Bind off 16 stitches and leave 18 stitches for stitch holder.
- Cast on (Right Front)—50 stitches.
- Row 1 (R Front)—Repeat 3 times and then 4 times.
- Row 2 (R Front)—Repeat 4 times and then 3 times.
- Collar, Step "b"—Rib stitch 18 stitches, 41 stitches from back stitching holder, and 18 stitches from the left front stitching holder. 77 total stitches.
- Collar, Step "d"—10 inches below.

Size 2XL:

- Supplies—**Yarn**—8 balls or skeins.
- Cast on (Back)—119 stitches.
- Row 1 (Back)—Repeat 8 times.
- Row 2 (Back)—Repeat 8 times.
- Shoulder Shape—Bind off 19 stitches and leave 43 stitches for stitch holder.
- Cast on (Left Front)—58 stitches.

- Row 1 (L Front)—Repeat 4 times and then 1 time.

- Row 2 (L Front)—Repeat 1 time and then 4 times.

- Should Shape—Bind off 19 stitches and leave 20 stitches for stitch holder.

- Cast on (Right Front)—58 stitches.

- Row 1 (R Front)—Repeat 4 times and then 1 time.

- Row 2 (R Front)—Repeat 1 time and then 4 times.

- Collar, Step "b"—Rib stitch 20 stitches, 43 stitches from back stitching holder, and 20 stitches from the left front stitching holder. 83 total stitches.

- Collar, Step "d"—10 inches below.

Socks

In the previous chapter, you tried your hand at making some cozy slippers to hug your toes, but now it is time to advance on to cover your whole foot and ankle with a lovely pair of knitted socks. The angles may appear to be difficult, but once you get used to the process, you will be knitting socks for all everyone you know. There are only a few things more comfortable than hand-knitted socks for your feet!

Simple Sock

Supplies:

Needles—US 1 or 2.5 mm, double pointed to circular are recommended
Yarn—light weight, fingerling weight, about 420 yards or about 3 balls
Extra—Stitch markers, a gusset for heel shaping

Gauge:

Gauge—32 S for 4 inches using stocking stitch

Instructions:

1. Create the cuff—

   a. Cast on 64 stitches, join working in the round and mark with a stitch holder to mark the start of the row.

   b. Knit 1, purl 2, and knit 2. Repeat 2-x-2 rib pattern (purl 2 and knit 2) until the last 3 stitches. Purl 2 and knit 1.

   c. Repeat Step "b" until the work is 1.5 inches.

   d. To ensure it is even on the second sock, write down the number of rounds the ribbing was worked.

   e. On the next row, knit 1, purl 3, and repeat the pattern for the length of the row.

   f. On the following row, slip 1, knit 3, and repeat the pattern for the length of the row.

   g. Alternate Steps "e" and "f" until the work measures 7 inches, ending on the second row, Step "f."

   h. To ensure it is even on the second sock, write down the number of slipped stitches.

2. Create the heel flap—

   a. Row 1—Knit 16, turn the work over, slip 1, and purl 31.

b. Make sure all your stitches are on one needle before beginning the next series.

c. Row 2—Slip 1 and knit 1, repeating the pattern across the row.

d. Row 3—Slip 1 and purl 31.

e. Alternate Steps "c" and "d" for 16 times.

3. Turn the heel—

a. Row 1—Slip 1, knit 18, slip, slip, knit, knit 1, and turn the work over.

b. Row 2—Slip 1, purl 7, purl 2 together, purl 1, and turn the work over.

c. Row 3—Slip 1, knit 8, slip, slip, knit, knit 1, and turn the work over.

d. Repeat Steps "a" through "c," adding 1 more stitch prior to every decrease until each stitch has been worked. This is about 20 stitches on the needle.

4. Create the sock—

a. Knit 20 stitches, pick up and knit 17 stitches. Place a stitching marker.

b. Knit 1, purl 3, and repeat for 32 stitches.

c. Pick up and knit 1. Place a stitching marker.

d. Pick up and knit 17 stitches to the gusset area.

e. Knit 10 stitches to the heel's center.

5. Create the gusset—

a. Row 1—Knit until 3 stitches until the stitching marker, then knit 2 together, knit 1, and slip the marker. Begin repeating knit 1 and purl 3 for the next 33 stitches. Slip the marker and knit 1, slip, slip, knit, and then knit the rest of the row.

b. Row 2—Knit to the first stitching marker and slip the marker. Begin repeating knit 1, purl 3 for the next 31 stitches, slip the marker, and knit to the end of the row.

c. Alternate Steps "a" and "b" until there are 32 stitches for the insole. This is 63 stitches altogether.

d. Continue working, shaping down until about 2.5 inches longer than the length you are wanting.

6. Create the toe—

a. Begin by knitting to the first marker and slip the marker. Repeat knit 1, purl 3 for 31 stitches, then knit 2 together, slip the marker, and knit to the end of the row.

b. On the next row, knit 1 across the row.

7. Create the toe shape—

a. Row 1—Knit across until 3 stitches remaining before the first marker. Knit 2 together and knit 1. When you slip the marker, knit 1, slip, slip, knit, and knit to within 3 stitches of the second marker. Knit 2 together, knit 1, slip the marker, knit 1, slip, slip, knit, and finish the row.

b. Row 2—Knit across the whole row.

c. Repeat Step "a" 4 additional times, decreasing each time until 16 stitches remain.

d. Knot across the first marker, changing the stitches on your needle so that the stitches for the instep are on one needle and the insole is on your other needle.

e. Trim the yarn, leaving a 16-inch tail.

8. Create/finish the sock

a. Using the yarn needle, sew the two sides together using a whipstitch.

b. Trim the ends and intertwine them into the project.

c. Repeat for the second sock.

Coffee Mug Coozies

For the coffee or tea lover in your life, give the gift of always keeping their hands protected and their coffee warm with a simple coozie. These can be made in all sorts of colors or combination. Have fun, add embellishments, and sip in style!

Simply Snug Coozie

Supplies:

Needles—US 10.5 or 6.5 mm
Yarn—4, medium, 1 ball or skein
Extra—snap fasteners

Gauge and size:

Gauge—13 S X 18 R for 4 inches using a stocking stitch
Size—Custom to fit your desired coffee mug in width, 4 inches long

Instructions:

1. Cast on 32 stitches.

2. Row 1—Knit across the row.

3. Row 2—Purl across the row.

4. Alternate Steps 2 and 3 until the project measures 2 inches, and you end on a purl row.

5. On the following row, knit 36 stitches across the row, including 1 stitch in the next stitch before knitting 7 stitches across.

6. Repeat Step 5 until the project measure 4 inches.

7. Bind off, trim the tail, and weave into the project.

8. Sew the snap fastener to the center of the side edges of the coozie.

Chunky Tie Coozie

Supplies:

Needles—US 10.5 or 8 mm **Yarn**—
6, super bulky, 1 ball or skein
Extra—yarn needle

Instructions:

1. Cast on 14 stitches.

2. Knit across the row, repeating for 6 rows.

3. Bind off knitwise, trim the edges, and weave into the project.

4. Using the yarn needle, take a piece of yarn and loop it through the center of the ends of the coozie. Wrap the coozie around a mug and tie the yarn ends to tighten it around the mug.

Coffee Coaster

Okay, this is not a coozie, but it is a stylish accessory for a cup made to protect your table from your mug! Plus, it is fun and a great way to practice your skills. What else can you ask for?

Supplies:

**Needles**—US 6 or 4 mm, double pointed or regular straight

Yarn—3, lightweight, about 25 yards
Extra—yarn needle, stitching marker

Gauge:

Gauge—11 S X 16 R for 2 inches using a stocking stitch. Gauge is not essential to this project.

Instructions:

1. Cast on 6 stitches and join in the round, placing a stitching marker to indicate the start of the row.

2. Row 1—For 12 total stitches, knit the stitch through the front and back loop.

3. Row 2—For 18 total stitches, knit 1 stitch through the front and back loops and then knit 1. Repeat this pattern until the 18 stitches.

4. Row 3—For 24 total stitches, knit 1 stitch through the front and back loops and then knit 2. Repeat this pattern until the 24 stitches.

5. Row 4—For 30 total stitches, knit 1 stitch through the front and back loops and then knit 3. Repeat this pattern until the 30 stitches.

6. Row 5—For 36 total stitches, knit 1 stitch through the front and back loops and then knit 4. Repeat this pattern until the 36 stitches.

7. Row 6—Knit 1, knit 1 stitch through the front and back loops, knit 3, and knit 1 stitch through the front and back loops. Repeat the pattern until 48 stitches.

8. Row 7—Purl the entire row.

9. Row 8—Knit 1, knit 1 together, knit 3 stitches through the front and back loops, and knit 2 together. Repeat the pattern until 54 stitches.

10. Row 9—Slip 1 and purl 8. Repeat the pattern for the entire row.

11. Row 10—Slip 1, knit 2 together, knit 4 stitches through the front and back loops, and knit 2 together. Repeat the pattern for 66 stitches.

12. Row 11—Slip 1 and purl 10. Repeat the pattern for the entire row.

13. Row 12—Knit 1, knit 2 together, knit 4 stitches through the front and back loops, knit 1, and knit 2 together. Repeat the pattern for 78 stitches.

14. Bind off purlwise. Trim the yarn and intertwine it into the project.

Chapter 5: Intermediate Knitting Preparation and Project

When I say purl, your hands automatically know how to move to make the stitch. When you hear "in the round," you know exactly what that means without looking it up. You have several "beginner" projects completed, and your friends and family are in awe over your new hobby. If you fall into one or two of those statements, pat yourself on your back. You can call yourself an intermediate knitter now!

Now that you have reached this stage, you are ready to push on further to gain even more new skills. The trick with this stage is that people will assume that if you have moved past the simple square and circle patterns, you can now tackle the wild and crazy projects, like brioche. Well, you may not be quite there yet, but with more intermediate project practice, you can be soon. Below are a few tips to help you advance a bit further and a few new projects to try out some of these new skills. Challenge yourself, have fun, relax, and enjoy the knitting ride.

8 Tips for Success as an Intermediate Knitter

1. Try your hand at making your own patterns

After you have done a few of the beginner patterns, you will notice that you can anticipate what the next step will be because it is always that way or you just realize it makes sense. In this case, you are ready to try your hand at making your own pattern. The beauty of this challenge is that it saves you the hours of reading through patterns, trying to find just the right one to make what you want with the skills and materials that you have on hand. A simple process for creating your own pattern is outlined below for you:

- Define the needles to be used in the project, ideally in both the US number and mm.

- Determine the yarn weight and length needed for the project. If you are uncertain of the number of balls or yardage, just keep track as you go along what you use so you can record it later.

- Measure the final size of the project. Make adjustments for larger sizes, if you want to get really fancy, otherwise just leave it at what you made

- Gauge is sometimes important and sometimes not, depending on the project. As you knit, measure the stitches and rows in a 4-inch square. This is the gauge. Record this information. If the project is smaller, measure the stitches and rows in a 1-inch square.

- If anything additional is needed to complete the pattern, like stitching markers, a yarn needle, or a fastener, make sure to write it down.

- When you are writing the instructions—

  - *Begin with how many stitches to cast on.*

  - *Try to be as clear and detailed as possible. Breaking it down by row is often the easiest method for presenting the steps.*

  - *If your project is going to increase or decrease, make sure to be clear about how many stitches it will grow or shrink by.*

  - *Watch capitalization, punctuation, and abbreviations. Stay consistent and clear.*

  - *If the pattern is going to involve multiple steps or pieces, use headers that are clear and precise.*

  - *If working in the round, make sure to mention stitch markers if you want them to be used.*

  - *Always end the pattern with the bind off instructions and steps on how to complete the project. Sometimes, you will need to sew the project together or add a closure, so include instructions on these steps as well.*

- If you are introducing a new or complicated stitch to your pattern, add images or diagrams to help the knitter understand what to do.

- If you want to show how to adjust sizing, include a schematic with the information.

2. *Check out new and challenging stitches*

In the previous projects, you were introduced to a few different stitches beyond the basics introduced in the very beginning. Just like you dove in and tackled those, now is the time to try your hand at even more advanced variations. Things like the "daisy" and "left twist" can sound scary, but when you break it down, you will see it is just another form of the basic knit, but it adds a new flair to an otherwise "basic" pattern. Think about the previous patterns in Chapters 3 and 4 and try replacing some of the stocking stitch rows with a few of these more intermediate stitches and watch how it completely transforms your project. Just this simple switch ramps up your project to "intermediate" level but keeps the majority of the pattern the same so you can create something you are more familiar with.

3. *Just keep learning, just keep learning, just keep learning...*

Take the time to celebrate your accomplishment of reaching this coveted intermediate status, but do not let yourself stay here forever. You have worked so hard to learn the skills necessary to get here. Keep challenging yourself to new projects. Consider projects with more pieces or steps that are made of all challenging stitches, or include materials that are not normally associated with knitting (think plastic or beads). What can it hurt to give it a go?

4. *Keep your stuff where it belongs*

If you do not have a place for all your knitting supplies, now is the time to find a storage solution. Keep your yarn neat and tidy. Make sure your needles stay paired together. Do not lose all your stitch markers or yarn needles at the bottom of a bag or drawer. By this point, you know what your favorite needles and supplies are. Clean out the "junk" that you did not like and proudly store those that you go to over and over again. If your supplies are easy to reach and well stored, you can get to them easily when you need them and know that they are in good shape when you are ready to go. For your yarn, consider storing it by color and weight so you can grab what you need when you need it. As you add more to the mix, find a place for it in your system, getting rid of something that does not fit anymore.

5. *Make the investment now*

When you first started, you were told to not buy the pricey stuff. Keep away from the expensive yarns. Try the more moderately priced needles first. Only buy a few things that you need to start. Now, you can splurge a little bit. Investing in an interchangeable needle set is a good idea for the intermediate knitter (that is you, now!). Buy a storage container that is made for more experienced knitters. Purchase those little accessories that will make knitting even easier for you. There is a host of options out there. Because you can accomplish so much and give such meaningful presents now, it is time to fork over the cash for the heirloom-quality needles and pricey cashmere yarn. You put in the time, now enjoy the reward.

6. *Find a community*

If you did not do this when you were starting out, now is the time to do it. Find a group of knitters of all skill levels to work on your projects with. Making sure it is a mix of people means that you can help the beginners get better because teaching is sometimes the best way to learn. Ask questions to the more advanced knitters. Those more advanced knitters may not be much more advanced than you, but they could have tried a technique or mastered a skill you want to learn and can be a handy resource along your journey. Coming into a group with only one skill level may seem like a good support group, but it will be hard to grow without the opportunity to learn and teach. Try to find a community that provides both for you. Plus, you are sure to have some good laughs along the way at all the silly mess up's that are made in all projects.

7. *Do not be afraid to fail*

You have made it this far; do not let the fear of a stitch or project hold you back now. This is the time to enjoy the challenge, but know you have the safety net of beginner projects to fall back on. Is the basket weave stitch not working out for you? Keep trying to master it. If you have a gift to give, create the project with a stitch you know and then go back to practice the basket weave.

8. *Try to read your stitches*

A true intermediate knitter will read their knitting like a book. You can look at your project and name all the stitches and techniques you did on each row, reading the row like a line in a book. This skill is not only incredibly impressive but it also lets you find mistakes and fix them quickly before it causes problems. As you keep practicing and repeating projects, you will become more and more familiar with the look of the stitch variations. It may seem impossible to identify this in the beginning, but by now, you should be getting kind of good at. As you move through this intermediate stage, you will get even better. Before you know it, you might be reading your knitting to your kids as a bedtime story.

Intermediate Knitting Stitches and Project

Hopefully, you are all hyped up at graduating to the intermediate level and are chomping at the bit to get going on a new pattern. Do not hold back! Try out one of these stitches in a previous pattern or give the pattern at the bottom a shot. Enjoy and keep those needles moving!

Stitches

Give some of these stitches a try in a previous project. They are fun and different. Consider replacing all the "beginner" parts of the pattern or just adding a few rows of one of these new stitches. They are sure to add some flair.

Quilted Diamond

1. Cast on 13 stitches at a minimum. Increase by multiple of 10 as needed.

2. Row 1—Repeat the pattern of purl 3 and knit 1, moving the yarn over and ending by knitting 1 stitch across the length of the row.

3. Step 2 creates a double row of stitching, and it adds 2 stitches for each repeat.

4. Rows 2 and 3—Purl 3 and knit 3, repeating the pattern across the row.

5. Row 4—Purl 3 together and knit 3, repeating the pattern across the row.

6. Row 5—Purl all the stitches across the row.

7. Row 6—Knit all the stitches across the row.

8. Row 7—Purl 1, knit 1, move the yarn over, and knit 1. Repeat this pattern across the row.

9. Row 8—Knit 2, purl 3, and knit 3. Repeat the purl 3 and knit 3 pattern until you reach the last 4 stitches. Finish by purling 3 and knitting 1.

10. Row 9—Purl 1, knit 3, and purl 3. Repeat the knit 3 and purl 3 pattern until you reach the last 5 stitches. Finish by knitting 3 and purling 2.

11. Row 10—Knit 2, purl 3 together, and knit 3. Repeat purl 3 together and knit 3 until you reach the last 4 stitches. Finish but purling 3 together and knitting 1.

12. Repeat Steps 2 through 11 as desired.

Pyramid

1. Cast on 9 stitches at a minimum. Increase by multiple of 8 as needed.

2. Row 1—Purl 1, knit 7, and purl 1. Repeat knit 7 and purl 1 to the end of the row.

3. Row 2 and all even rows—Knit 1 and purl 1.

4. Row 3—Purl 2, knit 5, and purl 3. Repeat knit 5 and purl 3 to the last 7 stitches. Finish with knit 5 and purl 2.

5. Row 5—Purl 3, knit 3, and purl 5. Repeat knit 3 and purl 5 to the last 6 stitches. Finish with knit 3 and purl 3.

6. Row 7—Purl 4 and knit 1. Purl 7. Repeat knit 1 and purl 7 to the last 5 stitches. Finish with knit 1 and purl 4.

7. Row 9—Knit 4, purl 1, and knit 7. Repeat purl 1 and knit 7 to the last 5 stitches. Finish with purl 1 and knit 4.

8. Row 11—Knit 3, purl 3, and knit 5. Repeat purl 3 and knit 5 to the last 6 stitches. Finish with purl 3 and knit 3.

9. Row 13—Knit 2, purl 5, and knit 3. Repeat purl 5 and knit 3 to the last 7 stitches. Finish with purl 5 and knit 2.

10. Row 15—Knit 1, purl 7, and knit 1. Repeat purl 7 and knit 1 to the end of the row.

11. Row 16—Knit 1 and purl 1.

12. Repeat Steps 2 through 10 again, as desired.

Waning Moon Shawl

Supplies:

> ***Needles***—US 5 or 3.75 mm
> ***Yarn***—fingering weight, 200 yards
> ***Extra***—blocking pins

Gauge and **Size**—

> ***Gauge***—19 S X 36 R in 4 inches, textured pattern after blocking
> ***Size***—70-inch long x 13 inches at longest point

Instructions:

1. Longtail cast on 12 stitches.

2. Knit 2 rows.

3. Knit the waning moon pattern:

    a. Row 1—On the right side, knit 1, yarn over, and repeat 2 times. Knit to the front and back of the stitch and then knit to the last 3 stitches. Knit to the stitch's front and back, yarn over, and knit 1, repeating yarn over and knit 1 again.

    b. Row 2—On the wrong side, knit 3, purl to the last 3 stitches, and knit 3.

    c. Row 3—Knit 1, yarn over, and repeat 2 times. Knit to the front and back of the stitch, then purl 1, and knit 1. Purl 2 and knit 2, repeating this pattern to the last 4 stitches. Purl 1, knit to the front and back of the stitch, yarn over, and knit 1, repeating yarn over and knit 1 again.

    d. Row 4—Knit 4 and purl 1. Repeat knit 2 and purl 1 until the last 4 stitches. Finish with knit 4.

    e. Row 5—Knit 1, yarn over, and repeat 2 times. Knit to the front and back of the stitch, purl 1, yarn over, slip, slip, knit, knit 2 together, and yarn over. Purl 2, yarn over, slip, slip, knit, knit 2 together, and yarn over, repeating this pattern to the last 4 stitches. Purl 1, knit to the front and back of the stitch, repeat yarn over, and knit 1 two times.

    f. Row 6—Knit across the row.

    g. Row 7—Repeat Row 1.

    h. Row 8—Repeat Row 2.

    i. Row 9—Repeat Row 3.

    j. Row 10—Repeat Row 4.

    k. Row 11—Knit 1, yarn over, and repeat 2 times. Knit to the front and back of the stitch. Knit 2 together, yarn over, purl 2, yarn over, slip, slip, and knit, repeating this pattern to the last 3 stitches. Knit to the front and back of the stitch. Finish with yarn over and knit 1 repeating 2 times.

    l. Row 12—Knit across the row.

4. Repeat Step 3 at least 9 times or until the shawl is your desired length.

5. Create the border:

    a. Repeat Rows 1 and 2 of the Waning Moon pattern.

    b. Row 3—Knit 3, purl to the front and back of the stitch, and knit 1. Purl to the front and back of the stitch 2 times and then knit 1. Repeat purl to the front and back of the stitch two times and then knit 1 until the last 4 stitches. Finish by purling to the front and back of the stitch and then knit 3.

    c. Row 4—Knit 5 and purl 1. Knit 4, purl 1, and repeat this pattern until the last 5 stitches. Finish with knit 5.

    d. Row 5—Knit 2, purl 2, and knit 1. Purl 4, knit 1, and repeat this pattern until the last 5 stitches. Finish with purl 2 and knit 3.

    e. Row 6—Repeat Row 4.

    f. Row 7—Knit across the row.

    g. Row 8—Knit 3, purl to the last 3 stitches, and knit 3.

    h. Row 9—Knit across the row.

    i. Row 10—On the wrong side, bind off knitwise.

CONCLUSION

Embracing Your Knitting Odyssey

Congratulations on reaching the conclusion of "The Simple Knitting Guide for Beginners." Your journey through these pages has been a transformative odyssey, weaving together skills, creativity, and the joy of crafting. As we reflect on the chapters explored and the stitches mastered, let's delve into the essence of your newfound connection with knitting and the boundless possibilities that lie ahead.

A Tapestry of Achievement

Consider the collection of projects you've undertaken—a vibrant tapestry of achievement that reflects your growth as a knitter. The hats, scarves, afghans, and various other items that now grace your space are more than mere objects; they are milestones marking your progress. Each stitch, cast on with intention, has contributed to a tangible manifestation of your creativity.

The Practice Projects that punctuated your learning served as bridges between theory and application. As you held those finished items in your hands, you not only witnessed the fruits of your labor but also experienced the gratification that accompanies the journey from novice to adept. The confidence gained from overcoming challenges and completing projects is a testament to your dedication and the unlimited potential within your grasp.

Beyond Yarn and Needles

The journey explored in this guide is not confined to the tangible realm of yarn and needles; it extends into the fabric of your daily life. Knitting is more than a craft; it's a practice that fosters mindfulness and relaxation. The rhythmic repetition of stitches becomes a meditative dance, allowing you to escape the hustle of daily life and immerse yourself in a world of creativity. The process of creating something beautiful with your own hands is a source of joy that extends beyond the finished product.

A Symphony of Stitches

From the foundational Cast On to the intricate Intermediate Knitting Stitches, you've learned to compose a symphony of stitches. Each technique, from basic knit stitches to more complex lacework, contributes a unique note to the melody of your knitting repertoire. The chapters of this guide have not only equipped you with skills but also fostered an appreciation for the nuances of the craft. As you look back at your journey, marvel at the diversity of stitches you've mastered, knowing that this knowledge opens doors to endless creative possibilities.

Crafting Connections

Knitting is more than a solitary pursuit; it's a craft that connects individuals across generations and cultures. As you continue on your knitting path, consider the rich tradition you've joined—a lineage of crafters who, like you, found solace, joy, and self-expression in the simple act of knitting. Whether you're crafting cozy blankets for loved ones or creating intricate garments, each project is a thread in the vast tapestry of human connection, linking you to a community that spans the globe.

Navigating Challenges

Your journey has not been without its challenges, and the occasional dropped stitch or unforeseen hiccup has likely tested your patience. Yet, it's within these moments of challenge that the true essence of knitting reveals itself. The ability to troubleshoot, adapt, and persevere is not just a skill for knitting but a valuable life lesson. In every challenge, there is an opportunity to learn, grow, and emerge with an even deeper appreciation for the craft.

The Continuation of Your Story

As we bid farewell to these pages, remember that your knitting story is far from over. The projects in this guide have provided a solid foundation, but your creativity knows no bounds. Feel empowered to explore new patterns, experiment with different yarns, and let your imagination guide your needles. The beauty of knitting lies in its adaptability—whether you're crafting practical items for everyday use or expressing your artistic vision through intricate designs, the possibilities are as vast as your imagination.

A Grateful Farewell

In closing, I extend my deepest gratitude for allowing this guide to be a part of your knitting journey. It has been an honor to accompany you through the exploration of stitches, projects, and the boundless creativity that knitting unlocks. As you continue to knit your story, may each stitch be a reminder of the joy, patience, and artistry woven into the fabric of your life.

So, with a heart full of gratitude and needles poised for the next project, I bid you a fond farewell. May your knitting adventures be filled with inspiration, warmth, and the pure joy of creation. Until our paths cross again in the vast world of crafting, happy knitting!

Crafting Memories and Traditions

As we bid adieu to this guide, consider the potential for knitting to become a cherished family tradition. The blankets, scarves, and handmade items you've created can serve as heirlooms, passed down through generations. Imagine the joy of wrapping your children, grandchildren, or loved ones in the warmth of a knitted piece, knowing that it carries not only the coziness of yarn but also the love and skill invested in its creation. In knitting, you've found not just a hobby but a way to craft enduring memories and traditions.

Finding Serenity in Stitches

Throughout your journey, you've likely discovered that knitting is not merely a hobby but a form of therapeutic self-care. The rhythmic motion of the needles, the feel of yarn slipping through your fingers, and the focus required to create each stitch contribute to a sense of mindfulness and serenity. As life presents its challenges, you now have a refuge in your knitting—a space where you can find solace, express your emotions, and create beauty amid the chaos. Your knitting needles become tools of self-discovery and resilience.

Sustainable Crafting

In an era where sustainability is at the forefront of our minds, knitting offers a unique opportunity to engage in eco-friendly crafting. By choosing quality, natural fibers and embracing the art of making instead of consuming, you contribute to a more sustainable and mindful approach to fashion and lifestyle. Your creations tell a story not just of creativity but of conscious choices, reminding us all of the beauty that can be cultivated with sustainable practices.

Building a Community

The knitting community is vast, diverse, and welcoming. Whether you've joined knitting circles, participated in online forums, or shared your creations on social media, you've likely experienced the camaraderie that knitting enthusiasts share. The exchange of ideas, tips, and stories fosters a sense of connection that transcends geographical boundaries. As you continue your knitting journey, consider reaching out to fellow knitters, sharing your experiences, and building connections that extend beyond the stitches on your needles.

The Artistry of Imperfection

In knitting, as in life, imperfections are an integral part of the journey. Dropped stitches, unexpected twists, and variations in tension are not flaws but unique aspects that make each piece distinctly yours. Embrace the beauty of imperfection, for it is within these quirks that the character and authenticity of handmade items come to life. Your knitting is a canvas where perfection takes a back seat to the joy of creation, and each "mistake" becomes a signature of your personal style.

A Canvas for Personal Expression

As you reflect on the projects completed and the techniques mastered, recognize that your knitting is a canvas for personal expression. The color choices, stitch patterns, and project selections are a reflection of your unique style and preferences. As you continue to explore new patterns and techniques beyond the pages of this guide, let your creativity flourish. Knitting is not just a craft; it's a means of expressing your identity, telling your story, and creating items that resonate with your individuality.

Beyond the Final Page

As we close the final page of this guide, remember that the end of one project marks the beginning of another. Your knitting journey is an ever-evolving story, and the skills acquired here are stepping stones to even greater creative heights. The patterns and projects within these pages are a launchpad for your imagination. Feel the freedom to experiment, innovate, and create your own designs. The world of knitting is vast and boundless, and each new project is an opportunity to push the boundaries of your skills and discover the depths of your creativity.

Gratitude for the Journey

In expressing gratitude for this shared journey, let it be known that your commitment to learning and creating has enriched the world of knitting. The tactile beauty of your creations now resides not only in your home but in the shared experience of all who embark on the knitting adventure. With heartfelt appreciation for your time, dedication, and passion, I extend warm wishes for a future filled with endless stitches, creative endeavors, and the pure joy that comes from knitting your own unique story. Until we meet again on the next page of your knitting journey, happy knitting!

Made in United States
Troutdale, OR
12/23/2024

27226695R00091